Migration

poems by

Cynthia Robinson Young

Finishing Line Press
Georgetown, Kentucky

Migration

ACKNOWLEDGMENTS

"Legacy" first appeared in *Across the Generations Anthology, Volume I*
My Father on His Deathbed" first appeared in the *Chattanooga Writer's
Guild 2015 Anthology*
"Nancy Beal-1820" first appeared in *Sixfold, Summer 2016* Issue

Publisher: Leah Maines
Editor: Christen Kincaid
Cover Art: Imara Young
Author Photo: Jasiri Harper
Cover Design: Leah Huete

Printed in the USA on acid-free paper.
Order online: www.finishinglinepress.com
            also available on amazon.com

Author inquiries and mail orders:
Finishing Line Press
P. O. Box 1626
Georgetown, Kentucky 40324
U. S. A.

Table of Contents

PROLOGUE: Message from Egururu

We don't see a shadow unless it's already been cast.

We saw our elders passing through the Valley of the Shadows,
the Shadow of death. We smelled decaying flesh, saw
bloated bodies. We recognized them nonetheless,
our mothers and fathers, our aunts and uncles, our babies unborn.

The ocean Atlantic was transformed.
It is the River Styx, running crimson, running
Blood Red. We see our reflections in the water.
We want to turn away.
We cannot. We have to look.
We have to
see.

Charon is disguised as Slave trader,
captaining the Middle Passage. He has stocked his ship
with desperate souls. We are praying for ascension, to fly,
but if not to fly, to die and be lifted
up and away. We pray
for death descending. We fling
the only thing left. Do we not own our lives? We fling them overboard,
into the warm water grave. The waves wait patiently
for us. The rest of us remain below,
buried in the bowels of the ship's living hell.
......

While George Washington was forging a new nation,
our elder parents were birthing the firstborn of our American family.
Her name was Egururu.
Our blood runs though Nigeria, Cameroon, Ghana, Cote D'Ivoire,
and here, in America.

Through tobacco and cotton fields, through thick and thin treed forests
our elder father, our elder mother, they found
each other, their bodies, their spirits came together,
warming the North Carolina soil.

It was here Egururu was born
and given the only gift she could keep—her name.
Not caring about the gift, her master gave her his chosen one
and she was reborn Charity
without even a surname until she married and
 became a Gatling only because her husband
was owned by one.

My name is Egururu,
no matter what they call me.
When you say my name, you tell my story.
So she told all of her children about the Shadows.
And we repeated it to our children, and so on,
and so on. And now,
come closer…
for we are telling it to you.

CHAPTER 1:
Nancy Beal—1820: 3rd Paternal Great-grandmother

I. Census

I found you
hidden in the Archives
in a census. Did they even let you
give your name?
Who asked the questions,
and who gave the answers that would define your life
two centuries later,
leaving me so little to understand who you really were?

Nancy.
You have a great, great, great-granddaughter who
carried your name into a generation
where there are no slaves such as you were...
She dances to tribal rhythms embedded
in Hip Hop, in Jazz, in melodic refrains
you might have hummed unconsciously
as you toiled in a hot North Carolina field,
or baked in a humid southern kitchen,
careful not be to overheard,
determined to remain silent when the overseer passed,
lest it be mistaken
for contentment.

II. History Class

Eighty years is a long time to have to live.
Nancy was born into a path
someone else had chosen,
a path no one in their right mind would choose.
So why did my fourth grade teacher tell us Black people did?
She said, "Negroes were swinging from trees like Tarzan,
because that's what they do in Africa!" We would have
done anything to get away from living like savages, "because that
is what you were!"
To hear her teach it, we must have run to the slave ship,
pushing our own Elders out of the way,
to be the first in this new land of dignity.

I didn't believe it at first, but there was a picture,
right on page 239, an illustration of this degradation,
so how could it not be true?
My cheeks burned red under my brown skin,
while the White students sat straighter
as the Black students slumped
lower.
I had no more questions. Being a slave was our destiny,
and they even got God to agree
as they cut and pasted through the Bible to show us.

III. Tell the Truth

Nancy did not fight to get on a ship
to be shackled for months,
stacked on other human beings
like Lincoln Logs. She was born here
in Rich Square, North Carolina,
when cotton saved the state from death, never minding
if they were killing her, fingers torn and bloody, her back,
bent over so many hours, it was hard to stand up straight
at the end of the day, at the end of her life.
She was sacrificed to give
North Carolina its thriving life.

Eighty years was not a long time for Nancy Beal to live,
but from 1820 to 1900,
thirty years must have felt like sixty,
and at eighty, she must have felt like a matriarch from the Old Testament.
It's not hard not to imagine her
catching that first glimpse of Glory,
singing "Hallelujah" louder than the angels.

IV. Two Trajectories.

They say that Nancy shared the same ground
as the Wright brothers while they toiled to take flight.
Is "toiled" the right word to use
when, after their bellies were filled,
they could lay on their backs at night,
look at the stars, ponder thoughts more lofty than
"when will the whip stripes heal on our backs
for not toiling hard enough?"

They say that Nancy shared the same ground as the Wright brothers,
but did she share the same ability to dream?
To be able to take off like a bird,
to soar above her life to freedom,
to land in an Eden that fed instead of starved
her imaginings?

V. Shared Stories

In the 1870 Census
you were fifty years old, living
with your four children, ages five to twenty.
The Fuente family is there too,
with ages so scattered, I have come to believe
they are not related to anyone but a slave owner
who distributed his name like a passport,
and when he sold them to another plantation,
no one bothered to change their names.
"Let them keep it" And so it was all they owned.
So there they were, the Fuentes and the Beals
together when the Census Taker came, related
only by the fate they shared.

CHAPTER 2:
Sarah Beale—1852, 2nd Paternal Great-grandmother

I. Family Tree Cut Down

We take our husband's names.
That's the way it's always been. In the Bible
Sarah called her husband "lord".
And in the eyes of God they were
co-heirs. Abraham was the Father of the nations,
and Sarah was our mother.

My question is,
Sarah Beale, are you my great great grandmother?
I found you with your mother, and then I lost you
among misspellings and multiple last names. Are you
The "Sarah Joney" who gave Mary away to Allen
because you were her mother, or are you "Sarah Beal"
her oldest sister, who, at twenty years, could have been either,
but the Census Taker didn't notice? Did you marry
William Jones? He was your age, and you could have
created a life together, even if you didn't want to give your daughter
his name.
Did you want just something
for yourself?

II. Now I Know

When you were thirty two, your little sister, Annie, married.
I think he was a nice man, that Silas Bush.
He had a father and a mother, whose names you knew—
Not just "Ma" and "Pa" but
Peter and Viney Lambertson Bush, a treasure now,
with all the elders gone,
and no one to ask but a website of strangers.
Now, I know that your father was William, and although
he was missing from the Census when you were twenty,
he isn't gone. I have a family of names,
fathers, not lost to their children,
husbands and wives, not lost to each other,
and so now,
not lost to me.

III. Erasure

Where were you when your sister died?
She must have treated him well, because Silas couldn't live
without a wife.
I hope it was about who *she* was,
and what she was to him, that he married again.
Young enough to be his daughter, this new wife was.
I can only wonder what was the talk going around about *that*?
Your mother had her hands full,
too full to be anything more than his mother-in-law. There were eight
new children! Had Annie birthed them all, then, exhausted, rose no
    more?
A year later, in walks Millie Jacobs
and there is a marriage,
she was just twenty two, only five years older than Mollie, the eldest.
Were they like sisters, Millie, and Mollie?
Did Millie try to prove she was elderly enough for her role of wife and
    mother?
Or did Grandma Nancy reign as matriarch,
having lived so long in those shoes praying, "Jesus, take me,"
that she didn't know how to set her power aside?
Names and dates lay silent, unable to record the stories
that only an ancestor, long gone
could tell me.

IV. Failed Revision

This is not looking good.
Your daughter Mary is here,
you and she, only 15 years apart.
Someone has listed you as her sister
when clearly you are not.
Were those dark days for you,
caring for a newborn
when you were not nurtured, not finished
growing up, yourself?

V. My Revision

I want to imagine you
standing behind your daughter, Mary,
under draping Wisteria,
with happy tears in your eyes!
You are the mother of the bride,
and the sound of fiddles and banjos duel and harmonize,
the fragrance of lilacs compete with the aroma of a wedding banquet,
none of the food cooked in The Kitchen House by you.

I want to imagine you, Sarah, not afraid
because of your belief in the future,
because of your hope for deliverance,
the war that divided this land is really over. And now I imagine
this is your wedding benediction:
may Mary never fear any separation from her beloved husband,
except in death, and even in passing,
may his eyes close as in sleep,
may he not die with eyes wide open,
with fear and terror
the last thing he sees,
as the eyes of so many Black men
before him.

VI. Small Triumph

Is it courage to believe in love in the midst
of suffering,
hard work from sun rising up until it set down again?
Sarah already had a daughter—she, only 15,
and still with her mother, Nancy.
But then, here it is! At twenty-eight, a union before God,
with a man named William Jones,
legally recorded in the North Carolina Marriage Records,
a paper trail that reminds me:
gravity can pull us to hope,
and hope to love, even in suffering so evil, so vile,
that all we have is our hope
and our love guiding us.

CHAPTER 3:
Mary Beale—1865, Paternal Great-grandmother

I. In Her Words

We grew up together,
Mama Sarah and me
and got married only a year apart.
I left her to finally care for her children herself.
"Don't call me Mama, I'ma leave here one day!"
I kept tellin' them,
but my sisters and brothers didn't believe me.
"Where you gonna go?" they asked. Well it been just me and them,
and their other mama, living just with ourselves
for so long.
I remember my granny,
how she up and left with Aunt Annie,
Probably because there was a man in the house
who might could take care of them better
than a bunch of women
could take care of each other.

Sista Allis was nine now,
almost all grown up,
far as I'm concerned. "You don't wanna know what all
I had to do at your age, Allis! Don't be cryin'! You big enough!"
So when Allen came
and said he wanted to marry me, I was ready.
I told Mama, "I'm your daughter, Mama, but
I gotta have my own life."
And now we both married women.
We came up together
like sisters. Now we together
all grown up.

II. Grief Don't Stop

It is not a big deal
I am now a "Gatling,"
that this land we workin' is ours.
A deed say we Gatlings
own this here land. But I'm thinkin' it might own me.
I was born when the Civil War ended.
I ain't a slave,
but I might as well be.
This living is as hard as it always was.
But Allen keep saying the toilin' is for us now.
It don't matter what Allen think we own. There ain't nothing
the White Man can't take back.

III. There's a Midnight Train

Standing over her husband's grave, she whispered,
"I told you there is more ways to kill black folk
than whippin' or hangin' em. They will not
do to me
what they did to you."
So she did the best she knew how. To escape the South
had always been her dream. There is no place she knew to go
where a woman will not risk her life anyway.
So she chose the place she wished to die—
not be in the place where her ancestors blood ran
through the veins of the southern soil,
not where their groanings could still be heard on a windy night.
Her children were grown now,
and could do for themselves.
It was time.

IV. Changing the Story

When I die
they will not find me in the Gatling graveyard.
There were so many of you. Where are you now?
I take my bones and my spirit to the North with me.
I want to take my children,
and my children's children,
because I will not return.
Never been any rest for me here.
Why do you think rest will happen in death?
Not here, not in this place.
I have picked the last piece of cotton,
I have seen the last Black man, the last Black woman
hanging from a tree.
I want a different eulogy when I die.

V. March 1965: Centurion

The newspaper reporter called me "Mary Glover."
It has been my name for so many years,
I almost forgot I was a Gatling, and before that, a Beale.
Then the next minute I remember a hundred years ago like I remember
　　yesterday.
I can still see street lamps instead of street lights,
envision forests where there are tall graffiti decorated housing projects.
I told that reporter I was a chambermaid.
My great-grandchildren don't even know what that is. I am full of stories
no one knows they need to hear—
not yet,
not until it is too late
to hear me tell them.
They will be buried with me in this cold, Northern winter earth..

I married a Glover, so now a Glover is who I am.
I never gave that reporter another name. My granddaughters don't even
　　know
all the women I was—
A "Beale" as a powerless child,
a "Gatling" as a dutiful wife, mother, and sharecropper,
a "Glover" as an independent woman
now writing my own life's script.

A Place To Lay Their Heads

Mary Beale Gatling,   1900

Mary told anyone who would listen
that if she didn't leave the South,
it would be the death of her,
and even knowing that her blood was running
through the veins of her children and grandchildren,
and that generations of her people
buried in this god-forsaken earth
was not enough
to keep her here.

She discovered that when she left
and not a moment before,
her heart could sing again!
The man she loved, dead now,
the only one who anchored her,
a love that chained her more
than any rusty shackle any White man could use to hold her down .

Mary Turner,   1899-May 19, 1918

Eighteen years after my great-grandmother left,
 over 500 people, Free men and Free women
 quickly grabbed who and what they had

and decided to follow her because of a single fact:
if they stayed in the South, they would live as though dead anyway.
Mary Turner was their last straw.

When she spoke with a passion a Black woman wasn't supposed to have
and asked for the justice she wasn't supposed to deserve,
a White mob decided to "teach her a lesson."
Why, to them, her husband wasn't even a full human being,
but an animal, a beast of burden,
nobody worth trying to go around to avenge the death of.

Feet tied together,
hung upside down,
lit with gasoline,
on May 19th
they set a 19 year old woman on fire,
and then, while hanging on to her life and the life
 of her unborn baby,

she could feel a knife cutting through to her womb,
heard her baby cry out as he fell to the ground,
saw him stomped on and crushed underfoot like a cockroach,
before her squinted eyes, stinging
from the smoke of her own flesh.

Mary Beale Gatling Glover, 1865-1968

Mary Beale lived over 100 years,
kept alive by the scent of freedom.
Every time she opened the windows
it blew in, lifting her arms in thankfulness.

She would have traveled to this freedom by foot
if she had to. What is a thousand miles
if it meant she would live?
It is not new.
It had been done
time and time again.

*Title from Forehand, Charles Tyrone. "A Place to Lay Their Heads." Maryturner.org. retrieved 4/12/2016.

CHAPTER 4:
Ransom & Ammie Davis—1863 and 1878, Maternal Great-grandparents

Ransom said he would never go back
to Georgia. He barely escaped with his life
the first time. He ran
because they thought he had killed
a White man who deserved it,
but back then the White Man never
got what he deserved.
There would be hell to pay if
Ransom had done what he thought
he did, and he and his whole family
would pay for it. So late one night
they boarded The Midnight Train,
away from Georgia,
Ammie and all their little ones,
and Ransom promised he'd come later.
Come to find out,
the White man was just knocked unconscious,
and now they were stuck in Newark, New Jersey,
for nothing, raising kids in a land of concrete and cement.
From her kitchen window at the top of the high rise,
Ammie could see
the New York skyline, but no further.
Ransom already knew that
and had stopped looking.

"I was working so hard, I couldn't tell slavery was over."

She held the scope of our family's history
 in the lines of her face.
I never saw her smile.
She spoke, but so seldom,
I can't recall her voice.

I remember nothing sweet or pretty,
except the flowers on her bib apron,
her uniform from sun up until she lay her body down.

I emptied her chamber pot,
fetched her spit cup for her tobacco,
washed her back, the only part of her still soft,

rolled pink "flesh colored" stockings up
her tired Black legs, her feet so leathery, it was
like she'd never worn shoes at all.
Is this my future I'm holding
 in my hands?

Granny sees the question in my eyes
and thrusts her foot forward, proudly,
knowing I can never do what she did to earn them.

CHAPTER 5:
Theosa Davis—1908-1992, Maternal Grandmother

No Turning Back

Theosa couldn't forget some things about the South,
the bitter rot of her life there, the scent of powerlessness
because she could still detect the stench of it in the North.
To hear her stories, I used to think she had been
a real slave.
"Might as well have," though she didn't mean it. The work was hard
    though,
always was,
and she never saw the Sabbath rest come for her.
And what she couldn't remember about the South,
her brothers did. They lost their brother in a chain gang
and she wanted me to name my son after him
but wouldn't tell me of the healing power a new little Derek
would have wrought. Because if I'd known,
if someone had just told me,
I would've done it.

She died without a line of fear or worry in her face,
never smelling the odor of the South again.

CHAPTER 6:
Gene (1926-1962) & Thelma (1930-1998), Parents

My father and mother went
as far as Baltimore before
they were reminded of the South.
They couldn't find a place to eat or to stay
 because they were
"Colored."
My father wouldn't stand for it,
it was their honeymoon,
but my mother pulled him back, reminding him
"This is America!, not France or Germany.
This is our war, this is how it was, and is,
 and will be."
So they got back in their car and came
back to New Jersey, and found
a diner to celebrate peacefully,
no blatant neon flash of prejudice
lighting up the predawn sky.

My Father on His Deathbed

…except he didn't have one.
His deathbed was an alley street,
far away from comfort.
He was abandoned,
lonely,
confused, staring at a needle
he had anchored into his arm,
not meaning to draw his life out. Staring into streetlights
until they become stars, he
wonders what will happen next
in a world he believed he created with his family, and now
believes
the drugs have destroyed.

I, on my twin bed,
across from my sister,
hear the doorbell ring at 4 in the morning,
see it is still dark as the night before,
recognize even then
the sound of the insistent knock
of Death's Messenger.

My mother, in her empty marital bed,
reaches out
to no one, then awakens
to grief
and an expectancy of
this visit,

these policemen,
this news
this ending
that was always on its way to
our doorstep.

Legacy

I lie in bed, awake, alone, and think about the past—
the hollow knock, the phone call in the night.
The water drips, the rhythm falls like heartbeats in a glass.

The day is like a photograph, when we stood upon the grass.
The sun glared as I stared up at his height.
I lie in bed, awake, alone, and think about the past.

His actions were abrupt that day, his words were low and fast.
The coins he gave me sparkled in the light.
The water drips, the rhythm falls like heartbeats in a glass.

He never gave a hint that day that it would be his last.
Was I too young to sense a strained goodnight?
I lie in bed, awake, alone, and think about the past.

White tombstones bordered brown tear-stained faces huddled in a mass.
Mom grabbed my hand and held my fingers tight.
The water drips, the rhythm falls like heartbeats in a glass.

He left some debt, some clothes, a car, a saxophone of brass,
a fear of knocks and phone calls in the night.
I lie in bed, awake, alone, and think about the past.
The water drips, the rhythm falls like heartbeats in a glass.

Visit from My Mother
-After Bill Brown

The fragrance of her perfume woke me in the night.
her spirit now untethered from her body,
her body not yet returned to the dust of earth.

Where did you go?
"To Heaven, where the angels sing."
Where did you go?
"To meet with God to give Him an answer."

Why did you come back?
"To tell you not to worry."
Why did you come back?
"Because I didn't want to leave."

Why did you leave?
"I made bad choices."
Why did you leave me?
"Because my days were never mine to number."

How do I go on?
"Love the people who have hurt us.
How do I go on, now?
"Love the people who *will* hurt you. They are human, just like you."

EPILOGUE: Migration

I live here now, in the South,
unbelief repented of, my blindness now sight.
The Elders told me our oral history,
and I know now
their stories never stretched into drama,
their tall tales into lies.
I sense the spirit of my ancestral past in me,
again subservient, powerless, sometimes
fearful for my own life, spared
because "You ain't from around here, are ya?"
Because I don't know
all the southern codes, the unspoken ones
deeply dug into the psyche
of every southern Black person who never boarded the train, the bus
headed anywhere but here, never shook
the red clay dust off their feet.

Still, it is a prodigal homecoming, my senses full of familiar history
resonating like long forgotten Blues, tunes hummed to comfort me,
like the murmur of southern secrets laced in Spanish Moss,
whispering among the whippoorwills,
the southern hospitality of eyes meeting, a stranger
but still neighborly enough to say "Hey!"
I find my family's everyday supper
chronicled on every *Meat and Threes* menu,
I see Aunt Seola's treasured northern vegetable garden
in most any backyard plot of land,
and I know my family missed the South— know it
in the way Grandma Theosa would lie,
spread eagle on the grass
wherever she found a patch big enough to rest in,
and pick fresh green beans and tomatoes

from her sister's garden in Long Island,
back gracefully bent, fingers nimble and brisk,
like she never complained even one day of arthritis.

They will not want me back here,
but they will envy me.
They will not say "You are courageous,"
but they will covet my foolhardy spirit.
They will not say "Traveling mercies!"
but they will pray for me,
that I find our family's space in the South,

I am a bird migrating south, soaring
in sultry air, resting
in lush viridescent trees, back
in my family's
second homeland.

Will I be free enough to reclaim
what was good in their lives here, and brave enough
to confront the ghosts that chased them away?

 I don't think I have that much power.

But I know their demons.
I have seen them myself,
and I have to tell you
the task seems insurmountable—

but Grandma always hummed
as the choir sang,
many tired souls tapping out the rhythm

on that stained hardwood church floor:

"Nobody told me
the road was gonna be easy,
but I don't believe He brought me this far
to leave me."*

So I'll bring our stories
and add them to this collective table.

It's the most that I can do.

*James Cleveland: "I Don't Feel No Ways Tired" lyrics

Cynthia Robinson Young's bloodlines run through Nigeria, Cameroon, Côte d'Ivoire and Ireland. Her family migrated to Newark, New Jersey from Early, Georgia, Eufaula, Alabama, Rich Square, North Carolina, and Portsmouth, Virginia beginning at the turn of the 20th century. She returned to the South to attend college, where she met her husband, but after graduation, migrated to the San Francisco Bay Area where their eight children were born, and where Young pursued writing and became part of the writing community in Berkeley, and in San Francisco State University's MFA program. Years later, her family migrated back to the South where she is an adjunct professor of Special Education at Covenant College, and is a graduate student at the University of Tennessee in Chattanooga.

Her work has appeared in several journals including *Radix, the Thorn, Sixfold, Poetry South, the Songs of Eretz Poetry Review,* and *Catapula: a journal of Southern Perspectives,* and anthologized in two volumes of *Across the Generations,* and the forthcoming confluence of Women's Voices, a publication of *A Room of Her Own Foundation.*